THE MANAGEMENT OF CARDIAC DISEASE IN DOGS

Peter Darke BVSc, PhD, DVR, DVC, MRCVS
Specialist in Veterinary Cardiology.
Honorary Member of Faculty, Department of Veterinary
Clinical Studies, Royal (Dick) School of Veterinary Studies,
Summerhall, Edinburgh

HENSTON

Produced in association with
Intervet UK Limited

First published 1995

© Henston Ltd, 1995

ISBN 1 85054 103 5

Henston Ltd, The Chequers, 2 Church Street, High Wycombe, Bucks, England

Printed and bound by EJW Colour Print Ltd, Swindon, Wiltshire

CONTENTS

1   Introduction 1
2   Function of the heart and circulation 2
3   Heart diseases in dogs 5
    a) Congenital heart diseases 5
        Pulmonic stenosis 5
        Aortic stenosis 6
        Patent ductus arteriosus 6
        Septal defects 7
        Multiple conditions 8
        Valvular defects 8
        Other defects 8
    b) Acquired heart diseases 8
        Heart valve diseases 9
        Myocardial diseases 9
        Pericardial diseases 11
4   Heart failure 12
    Low-output failure 12
    Congestive heart failure 13
    Heart rhythm and irregularities 15
    Cardiac arrest 16
5   Diagnosis of heart diseases 17
    The clinical examination 17
    Further Investigation of heart disease ... 19
        Radiology ('X-Ray') 20
        Electrocardiography (ECG) 20
        Echocardiography (ultrasound scan) 22
        Doppler echocardiography 23
        Cardiac catheterisation 23
        Other tests 24
6   Treatment of heart disease and heart failure 25
    Specific (surgical) therapy 25
    Treatment of Congestive heart failure 26
        Diuretics 26
        Digitalis glycosides 27
        Vasodilators 28
    Treatment of severe pulmonary oedema 30
    Treatment for coughing 30
    Treatment for bradycardias 31
    Treatment for tachycardias 32
    Treatment for cardiac arrest 34
Appendix A 36
Glossary 37

PREFACE

As the range of treatment and management options increase for many animal diseases, more complex and detailed knowledge is required by all who participate in the patient's care. Cardiac disease in the dog, for example, can now be managed in circumstances where, in the past, the outlook was grim. This can only happen, however, if all involved in this care have a thorough understanding of the aims of treatment, the correct management, the likely outcome and, should the worst happen, how to resuscitate the compromised patient.

This excellent volume by one of the country's leading veterinary cardiologists, Dr Peter Darke, provides a comprehensive yet easily understood reference for vets, veterinary nurses and owners of the cardiac patient. The depth of understanding which can be gained from this should ensure the best of care for the cardiac patient, young or old, so leading, when possible, to a prolonged life of quality.

Allan J Henderson BVM&S, MRCVS
Editor

1 Introduction

The heart is a crucially vital organ without which your dog cannot survive. When heart disease is detected by a veterinary surgeon, whether following obvious signs of illness or as an incidental finding during a routine health check, it is usually rather worrying for those close to the patient. In recent years, however, great advances have been made in the understanding of heart disease in the dog and many treatment options are now available.

Heart disease is surprisingly common in dogs, representing about 5-10% of all the clinical cases seen by a typical small animal veterinary surgeon. Although some people may have witnessed heart disease in friends or relatives, the pattern of disease in dogs is usually rather different. Many humans have 'heart attacks' associated with disease of the coronary arteries (the arteries which supply blood to the heart muscle), but this is almost unknown in dogs. The heart diseases affecting dogs are less likely to give rise to sudden death.

When dogs have heart disease, they may need prolonged veterinary care, which requires the development of a close relationship and understanding between their owners and the attending veterinary surgeon if the patients are to have the best treatment available and enjoy the highest quality of life.

In dogs, heart disease may develop slowly or, alternatively, have been present from birth. Initially the patient may cope well but if the condition is serious, progressive heart failure is almost inevitable requiring careful and efficient nursing. As busy people may find it difficult to make time for this, a careful discussion between the vet and the owner is vital at the outset. This discussion should cover the nature of the disease, the care that may be needed, the likely cost and probable outcome.

This booklet attempts to explain the nature of the most common heart diseases seen in dogs, the techniques used to make a diagnosis, and the type of management and drugs that may be used in treatment. It has been prepared for the benefit of the owners, their vets and veterinary nurses in an attempt to improve the understanding of the role that each can play in caring for the cardiac patient. Although medical words are used, a glossary is provided to help people without training to understand the meaning of some of the more technical terms.

2 Function of the heart and circulation

The heart is obviously vital — if it stops, life rapidly ceases. It is a pump that ensures the supply of oxygen and vital nutrients essential for the maintenance of all body tissues.

Blood in the veins has had oxygen removed during its passage through the body, and it must pass through the lungs to have the oxygen replenished. Furthermore, as the nutrients are consumed by the body tissues, the blood collects the waste products of metabolism and transports them to the liver and kidneys where they are further metabolised and excreted.

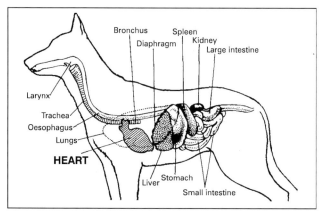

Position of heart in the dog

There are two 'sides' to the heart and circulation. The left ventricle is the main pumping chamber for the blood supplied to most of the body, whilst the right ventricle pumps blood to the lungs. Each ventricle is supplied from a receiving chamber (atrium) where the blood arrives at the heart from the circulation. The left atrium receives blood from the lungs, and the right from the body. Although the left ventricle, a thick muscular pump, has most work to do, both sides of the heart are vital, and depend on one another if they are to function efficiently.

Between the atria and the ventricles are the atrioventricular

2

valves. The one in the left side of the heart is known as the mitral valve, and that on the right, the tricuspid valve. The left ventricle pumps blood out through the aortic valve into the aorta, the main artery supplying the body, and the right ventricle supplies the lungs via the pulmonary artery through the pulmonic valve. These valves protect the ventricles against the high blood pressures present in the circulation and allow filling from the atria when the heart relaxes between beats.

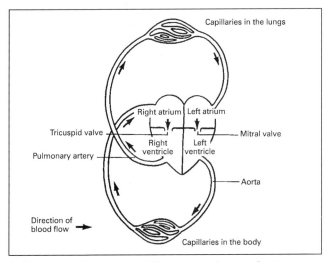

Schematic diagram of heart and circulation

The speed at which the heart pumps (heart rate) is variable, according to the body's requirements. The rate is controlled by special nerves from the autonomic nervous system which controls involuntary or unconscious activity in the body. Some of these nerves secrete adrenaline which is well known for its effects on heart rate during excitement, at exercise, or when frightened. The normal heart rate in dogs is very variable since it usually depends much on the animal's excitability. Most normal adult dogs have a heart rate between 60 and 140 beats per minute at rest although this is not constant since the heart tends to speed up and slow down quite markedly in time with the breathing. This is known as sinus arrhythmia.

The heart rate can easily be checked by feeling for the heart beat ('apex beat') just behind the dog's elbows.

As well as controlling heart rate, the strength of the heart beat may also be controlled by the autonomic nervous system. Blood

3

vessels, too, can be selectively expanded (vasodilation) or contracted (vasoconstriction), and this is another vital function in the control of the circulation. An example of how this controls circulation is that when extra blood supply is needed by the muscles during exercise, blood vessels in the intestines can be shut down.

Vasoconstriction, which occurs under the influence of the autonomic nervous system and the hormones angiotensin and vasopressin, is also vital in the control of blood pressure. When sensors (receptors) in the blood vessels detect a marked fall in pressure, mechanisms come into play to reduce the size of all but the most vital vessels (eg to the brain and the heart). This maintains the blood pressure in the vital organs. This is an excellent way for the body to compensate for sudden fluid loss such as occurs in acute haemorrhage or severe diarrhoea and so ensure survival. Circulatory fluid loss can also be restored by the kidneys.

3 Heart diseases in dogs

Heart disease can be congenital ie the animal is born with a defect, or it may be acquired later in life. Hardly surprisingly, the heart is subject to a degree of 'wear and tear' during its years of service since in the lifetime of a dog, it is likely to beat over 500,000,000 times. It is therefore a remarkably reliable pump and it is not surprising that from time to time it may cause problems!

Congenital heart diseases

Significant birth defects in the heart probably occur in about one in every 200 to 500 puppies born, although it is often not immediately apparent to the new owner. Most often, a 'murmur' (from turbulent blood flow) is found by the vet when the pup is taken for vaccination. Only in the most severe cases will the pup fail to thrive at this stage.

The conditions most commonly found in puppies at this stage of life are pulmonic stenosis, aortic stenosis and patent ductus arteriosus, although defects can occasionally be found in any of the heart valves and in the wall between the two sides of the heart (septal defects). Most of these defects are hereditary ie they can be passed through the genes to offspring, and affected animals should never be used for breeding.

Pulmonic stenosis

This is a deformity of the pulmonic valve which obstructs the flow of blood from the right ventricle to the lungs. In Britain, the disease is found most frequently in Spaniel type breeds, Boxers and miniature Schnauzers.

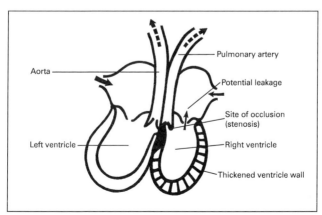

Pulmonic stenosis

Affected pups usually appear well at first, although their growth may gradually become retarded. Dogs with severe disease are often incapable of sustaining hard exercise without tiring or becoming breathless (dyspnoea). The obstruction can usually be relieved, but not easily cured, by surgery or by using a balloon catheter from the jugular vein through the heart. In this technique, the tip of a tube or catheter is passed from an external blood vessel to the site of the lesion where a balloon near the end is inflated to stretch the defect and allow improved blood flow.

Aortic stenosis

This defect, which causes obstruction to the flow of blood from the left ventricle, is becoming increasingly prevalent in dogs in UK and abroad. The breeds most frequently affected in the UK are from some larger breeds, including Boxers, Golden Retrievers, German Shepherd Dogs, Bull Terriers, Samoyeds and Rottweilers. Affected animals often appear to be normal in themselves but may appear weak or tired when exercised hard. The most alarming feature of severe disease, however, is that apparently healthy-looking dogs may suddenly collapse or die at exercise or when excited. Unfortunately, there is little reliable treatment for aortic stenosis.

Both pulmonic and aortic stenosis can cause heart murmurs that can be easily heard with a stethoscope, but definitive diagnosis and information about the severity of the condition in a particular patient can only be obtained after more sophisticated investigation (see Chapter 5).

Patent ductus arteriosus

The ductus arteriosus is the blood vessel which is used to by-pass the lungs of the pup before birth, while the lungs are still inactive.

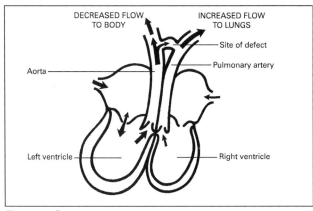

Patent ductus arteriosus

Normally, when the pup first breathes, the ductus should seal off. Sometimes, however, it remains open (patent), allowing blood to be pumped from the aorta directly into the pulmonary artery. This causes an overload of blood in the lungs since blood is being pumped both from the high pressure left and the low pressure right heart. This is described as 'left to right shunting' and can lead to breathing difficulties and/or heart failure at any time in the animal's life. The defect is found most frequently in German Shepherd Dogs and Cavalier King Charles Spaniels in the UK although it is one of the few lesions found in cross-bred dogs, and more often in bitches than in male dogs.

This disease is easily diagnosed by vets from the characteristic murmur it causes, and early detection is important: as the defect is easily corrected by skilled specialist surgeons.

Septal defects

The defect most frequently found in human babies, although less commonly in dogs, is the classic condition described as the 'hole in the heart'.

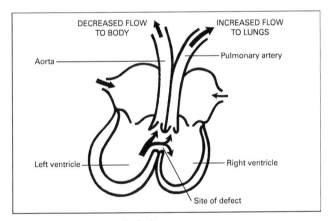

Ventricular septal defect

In this condition the two ventricles (ventricular septal defect) or atria (atrial septal defect) are not sealed off from each other. The abnormal flow of blood through the defect, as would be expected, is usually from the higher pressure left side of the heart to the low pressure right. As a result and as in patent ductus arteriosus (see above), the lungs become over-perfused with blood, particularly if the defect is large, leading to breathing difficulties and/or heart failure. More commonly in dogs, however, this defect is small and usually the animal is not particularly inconvenienced. The defect usually produces a murmur which the vet can detect by auscultation. In the UK this condition is found most frequently in West Highland White Terriers.

Multiple conditions

Multiple congenital lesions can also arise in dogs when more severe clinical complications can arise. If, for example, a very large septal defect is present and there is also some obstruction to the blood flow to the lungs (eg pulmonic stenosis), the flow of blood may be reversed ('right-to-left shunting'). This is a classic disorder described in humans as a 'blue baby'. Blood arriving at the right side of the heart from which oxygen has been extracted in the body, is pumped back into the aorta instead of the lungs, and is circulated again around the body without further oxygenation. Oxygen-depleted blood loses its red colour so bestowing a blue tinge to the skin (cyanosis). Affected animals do not grow well and become very easily tired and breathless if they try to exercise. The defect is fortunately rather rare in dogs as it cannot easily be corrected.

Other valvular defects

Either the mitral or the tricuspid valves, whilst more often affected by disease in old age (see later), can also be deformed at birth. They may leak badly, leading to breathing difficulties and heart failure early in life. Mitral valve 'dysplasia' is found frequently in English Bull Terriers, and a defect in either valve causes a heart murmur audible on auscultation.

Other defects

Many other abnormalities of the heart such as the defective positioning and formation of the major vessels can be found, but fortunately they occur only rarely in dogs. In some cases, the sac around the heart (pericardium) may be malformed and occasionally abnormal positioning of vessels may restrict the oesophagus as it passes the heart, so causing recurrent regurgitation of food.

Acquired heart diseases

Most heart disease seen in veterinary practice (95%) develops in adult dogs, and it usually affects one or more of three specific areas. These are the valves, the heart muscle (myocardium) and the sac which surrounds the heart (pericardium). Additionally, the way the heart beats, particularly the pumping of the ventricles and the rhythm, can be affected by many other metabolic disturbances not primarily related to the heart. These include hormonal diseases (eg thyroid deficiency); kidney failure and related hypertension; brain or nerve ('neurological') disease; anaemia or chemical disturbances.

Heart valve diseases

Heart valve diseases are found in many ageing dogs, particularly the smaller breeds such as Cavalier King Charles Spaniels, Chihuahuas, Lhasa Apsos, Miniature Poodles, Pekingese and Whippets. The valve 'leaflets' or flaps, particularly those of the mitral valve in the left side of the heart, thicken and lose their elasticity, leading to valve leakage ('incompetence' or 'regurgitation'). As this disease is usually slow to develop, many ageing dogs tolerate a leaking valve for months or years and are quite old before clinical effects are noticed. Cavalier King Charles Spaniels, however, are different in that they tend to develop disease earlier in life.

The first sign in any active dog developing mitral valve disease, is some slowing down during exercise, which may or may not be accompanied by breathlessness. Coughing, however, is usually the first obvious sign to be reported by owners of dogs with significant mitral valve leakage. When presented at the surgery, a heart murmur is usually easily detected when the heart is examined with a stethoscope.

With careful management in terms of exercise and diet (see later), many dogs will survive happily with this common disease for months or even years. Eventually, however, treatment for heart failure will probably be needed, probably for a prolonged period of time, and finally the heart may fail to respond even to this, leading to circulatory collapse.

Occasionally the tricuspid (right atrioventricular) valve is more severely affected. This may lead to the accumulation of fluid in the abdomen (ascites or 'dropsy'), gradual weight loss and generalised bodily deterioration.

Myocardial diseases

The heart muscle (or myocardium) is easily damaged by many diseases because of its relentless activity throughout life. For example, the muscle can be affected by inflammation ('myocarditis') with or without infection; it can be bruised in trauma such as road accidents; it can be poisoned; it can be invaded by cancers, or its function as a pump can be affected by chemical ('metabolic') disturbances in other parts of the body. Furthermore, in chronic heart failure it may become so seriously overloaded that it finally fails to pump effectively, leading to circulatory collapse.

One of the most important diseases of the heart muscle in dogs is dilated cardiomyopathy. In this disease, the heart muscle becomes weakened for unknown reasons, becomes slack and flabby, and fails to pump blood around the body effectively. Although the actual cause is not known, the onset of disease is often sudden, which may suggest exposure to some infection or toxic substance. However, it occurs only in a limited range of dogs from large and giant breeds such as Dobermans, Great Danes, Irish Wolfhounds, Newfoundlands and St Bernards suggesting additional breed related susceptibility. In addition, most affected dogs are male, and the disease can occur at almost any age. Although it affects mainly the larger breeds, it is occasionally seen in some slightly smaller breeds such as the Flat-coated Retrievers, Irish Setters, Old English Sheepdogs, and Cocker and Springer Spaniels.

Not only does this disease prevent the heart from pumping properly, but the electrical properties of the heart muscle cells (myocytes) themselves may also be altered. This often leads to disturbances of the heart rhythm ('dysrhythmias') further contributing to a loss of pumping efficiency.

Sadly, the prognosis for most dogs with dilated cardiomyopathy is poor. Eventual failure of the heart muscle leads to complete failure of the heart as a pump, and there is little that can be done to resolve the condition. There is considerable breed variation in response to treatment, since in Dobermans the long-term prognosis is usually grim even if they initially respond well to treatment, whilst with spaniels, the contrary is often true.

Early signs of the disease include loss of energy at exercise ('exercise intolerance'), breathing difficulties, coughing, weight loss, weakness and/or ascites. Sudden death is common after some weeks or months. Diagnosis is rather more difficult than for some other diseases because there may be no heart murmur, and a definitive diagnosis requires a heart scan using ultrasound (or echocardiography) (see later).

In some other diseases, the myocardium may become excessively thickened (hypertrophied). This can occur if there is an obstruction of one of the large vessels and the outflow of blood is obstructed (eg congenital aortic or pulmonic stenosis). Excessive pressure develops in the ventricle causing it to become hypertrophied as a result of the continually harder work it has to undertake. Hypertrophy can also occur with high blood pressure (hypertension), which is not nearly as common in dogs as in humans, or more rarely for no obvious reason (hypertrophic cardiomyopathy). What ever the cause of hypertrophic cardiomyopathy, filling of the heart chamber may be restricted and the myocardium may be starved of oxygen, leading to heart failure or even sudden death.

Pericardial diseases

The pericardium is the sac (bag) that surrounds the heart, and in normal, healthy animals it serves little useful purpose. If it becomes rigid or fills with fluid, however, then the ability of the heart to expand and fill between beats (diastole) will be compromised. Should this occur, it affects the thinner-walled right side of the heart to a greater degree than the more muscular left side, and this rapidly leads to weakness, breathlessness and ascites.

Pericardial disease can arise for various reasons. Cancers (neoplasia) may bleed (haemorrhage) causing a build up of fluid within the pericardium. More frequently, blood is found as a result of spontaneous haemorrhage which occurs for unknown reasons. This is described as haemopericardium and it occurs most frequently in Golden Retrievers and some other of the larger breeds of dog. If the accumulation of pericardial fluid, whether blood or other fluid (pericardial effusion), is diagnosed in time, the results of treatment are often very pleasing. Many effusions can be drained successfully, but more complicated surgery is sometimes needed to effect a cure.

4 Heart failure

The heart and circulation can compensate for mild disease if it develops slowly, for example with mild valvular incompetence, often for months or even years before the animal shows any signs of illness. This is particularly true of a lazy domestic pet which spends much of the day curled up asleep. Eventually, however, the heart may not be able to pump blood effectively. This is likely to be noted first at exercise and is described as 'forward' or 'low-output' failure. Poor circulation means that not only do the dog's muscles and lungs lack an adequate supply of oxygen and nutrients to sustain energetic exercise, but kidney function may also be compromised by an inadequate blood supply. In such circumstances, the kidneys react as they would to a sudden loss of blood and attempt to retain as much water and salt (sodium) in the body as possible. This leads to excess fluid in the circulation, which is described as 'volume overload' and so leads to 'congestive heart failure'.

Low-output failure

Low-output failure occurs most commonly with myocardial failure, but it may also occur with severe disturbances to heart rhythm (dysrhythmias). If the heart rate falls below 50 or exceeds 250 beats per minute, for example, or if there are frequent extra and uncoordinated beats not originating from the heart pacemaker (ectopic beats or fibrillation), signs of disease may be apparent. Similar signs may also be seen with the condition congenital aortic stenosis (see earlier). Signs of low output failure may not be limited to exercise intolerance, since affected dogs may show weakness or collapse, leading to unconsciousness, even when not unduly exerted. Such 'heart attacks' may resemble those seen in human patients, although unlike in humans, they are not usually related to coronary artery disease, which is more likely to be fatal. Coronary artery disease is almost unknown in dogs. With low output failure, many dogs have recurrent episodes of collapse yet show few long-term ill-effects (unlike some of their worried owners!), recovering promptly after each attack. There are many other causes of recurrent collapse in dogs e.g. epilepsy or low blood sugar (hypoglycaemia), and only a minority of all dogs which show weakness do so as a result of cardiac disease.

If collapse is due to low output failure, the dog usually develops a true faint — it will be still and lifeless and the colour of the tongue is likely to be pale. The dog may recover rapidly and be apparently fully well within minutes. In epilepsy and some other forms of fits ('seizures'), however, the dog is likely to go rigid at the start of the attack, then shake and paddle with the legs, and breathe heavily; the eyes usually show movement, and the tongue may be blue. Furthermore, the animal is often bewildered during recovery for minutes or even hours. It is worth noting details of the behaviour of a dog during episodes of collapse, to help a vet diagnose the likely cause. It is also worth checking the heart (by feeling the chest behind the elbow) for activity, rate and rhythm during the attack, if the situation does not cause too much panic! A vet can detect low cardiac output by detecting weakness in the pulse and pallor in the mouth which occurs as a result of the tightening of the small blood vessels (vasoconstriction), the body's reaction to low cardiac output.

Congestive heart failure

Congestive heart failure arises as a result of the excessive accumulation of fluid in the body due to inadequate cardiac function. As mentioned earlier, this fluid retention takes place at the kidneys, partly through the lack of adequate blood circulation. Congestive failure may affect mainly the left-side or the right-side of the circulation or it may be generalised. Congestive failure is regarded as a 'backward' failure, in which veins are distended by the inability of the heart to pump the blood into the arteries and away from the venous circulation, and as a result, fluid is 'squeezed' from the veins into the tissues as oedema.

Left-sided failure tends to be seen with disorders affecting predominantly the left side of the heart such as mitral valve disease, or patent ductus arteriosus (see earlier). A leaking mitral valve causes a build-up of fluid in the left atrium, which backs up into the veins of the lungs (pulmonary vein congestion). If this pressure builds up beyond a certain point in the veins, especially if heart failure occurs rapidly rather than insidiously, then fluid may be 'squeezed' into the lungs giving rise to pulmonary oedema. This causes rapid and laboured breathing (dyspnoea), even at rest, and the dog may become very distressed. Frothy fluid may even be seen at the dog's nose and may be coughed up. Dyspnoea is partly due to the poor transfer of oxygen from the air being breathed by the dog to the blood in its lungs as a result of the fluid in the lungs, but also because fluid-sodden lungs are stiff and fail to expand and empty properly. Severe pulmonary oedema is a serious state in which the dog may rapidly drown.

More commonly in dogs, coughing is a prominent sign of left-sided congestive failure, especially in mitral valve disease. This

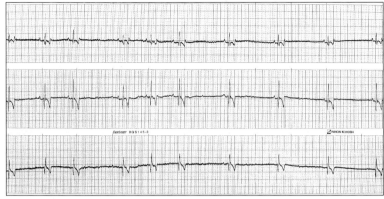

(1) ECG from a normal dog. The heart rate is relatively slow, there is regular irregularity (sinus arrhythmia), which is common in normal dogs, and the ECG shows no evidence of heart enlargement.

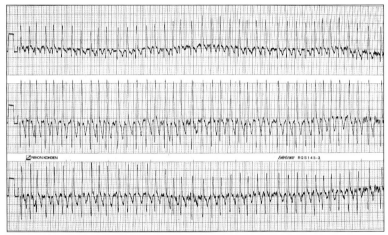

(2) ECG from an Irish setter with heart failure associated with dilated cardiomyopathy. The heart rate is very fast and irregular (with artrial fibrillation), and the waves of the ECG are large, indicating cardiac enlargement.

14

is partly because the large left atrium, overfilled with blood that has leaked back through the mitral valve, presses on small airways (bronchi and bronchioles) and partly because the small airways are swollen with fluid and partly collapsed. This often complicated by the fact that many ageing dogs have a degree of chronic bronchitis.

Right-sided congestive failure is associated particularly with tricuspid valve or pericardial disease. Increased back-pressure in the right atrium leads to increased pressure in the main veins of the body. Fluid is 'squeezed' into many body tissues, including the liver, intestines, and body cavities. Liver enlargement and ascites (fluid in the abdomen) are the cause of abdominal enlargement, and it is not unknown for owners of dogs with right-sided congestive failure to believe that their dog is merely becoming obese! However, close examination of the animal will often show that there has been considerable loss of flesh covering the bones and a general deterioration of body condition. The cause for this is uncertain, but it may be partly to do with the poor absorption of food as a result of oedema in the digestive tract.

Generalised congestive heart failure may also be seen in cardiomyopathies, which affect both sides of the heart, or following on at a later stage of either left or right-sided heart failure since both sides of the circulation are connected.

Heart rhythm and irregularities (see page 20)

The heart rate is normally controlled by specialised heart cells described as the pacemaker or sinus node. In dogs, this typically maintains the heart rate at between 60 and 140 beats per minute at rest. When the dog is excited, exercises, or has heart failure, however, the heart speeds up, mainly under the influence of adrenaline. Although this increases the actual amount of blood that the heart can pump around the body in a set time, this increase in rate (tachycardia) is at the cost of efficiency. The rapidly beating heart does not fill fully on each beat, and it consumes more energy and oxygen for the same amount of work. Tachycardia can also arise as a result of irritable damage to the heart muscle which causes it to take over control of the heart rate from the pacemaker and so beat faster.

Some tachycardias, diagnosed by ECG, are potentially dangerous in that they may precede ventricular fibrillation, a common cause of cardiac arrest. When beating at a grossly excessive rate, the heart does not fill properly, and it beats very feebly, producing a weak and rapid pulse. The heart rate in tachycardia can exceed 300 beats per minute in dogs. This may cause low-output failure (see earlier), and if the condition persists, may lead to congestive heart failure.

If the pacemaker itself is diseased, if some disorder of the brain or nerves impairs emission of nerve impulses, or if the pathway through the heart by which the nerve impulses are transmitted to the ventricles is diseased (heart block), then the heart may beat too slowly for the dog to sustain normal activity. In some cases of heart block, the pacemaker may lose control of the ventricles entirely. The heart then produces a 'rescue' or 'escape' rhythm from subsidiary pacemaking tissue in other areas of the ventricles. An escape rhythm is often in the range of only 30 to 60 beats per minute in dogs. This, again, may result in the development of low-output and/or congestive failure, and the dog is at risk of sudden death.

Cardiac arrest

Cardiac arrest, the classic 'heart attack' that results in sudden death, can occur in dogs but, as discussed before, is not found nearly as frequently as it is in humans, owing to the rarity of coronary artery disease. Cardiac arrest may arise when the heart actually stops or when there is 'fibrillation', an uncoordinated writhing of the ventricles outwith the control of the heart pacemaker.

Signs of cardiac arrest include cessation of breathing and true and deep unconsciousness. The tongue may initially be pale but later it is likely to turn grey or blue. The pupils of the eyes may become widely dilated. In event of cardiac arrest, resuscitation should be carried out much as it is in humans (see appendix A).

Diagnosis of the type of cardiac arrest requires an ECG either during the attack or following recovery.

5 Diagnosis of heart diseases

A thorough clinical examination by a vet in practice remains the mainstay in the diagnosis of cardiac disease, although confirmation of the actual cause is likely to require much more sophisticated and specialised investigation. This is necessary not only to provide detailed information about heart function but also to eliminate other diseases which may mimic the same symptoms. For example, dyspnoea can be a prominent sign of serious, left-sided heart failure but can also a sign of numerous different forms of respiratory disease, such as pleural effusions (fluid in the chest) or cancer. Differential diagnosis in this case is most easily resolved by radiology (X-Ray) which will usually show up the presence (or absence) of pulmonary lesions. Coughing, similarly, is not just a sign of heart disease since it can also be caused by cancer, bronchitis, 'lungworms' and even the inhalation of 'foreign bodies' such as twigs or barley awns. Coughing is often best investigated by bronchoscopy where a fibre-optic tube is passed down into the lungs under general anaesthetic in order to visualise the airways. This requires fairly specialised equipment, however, and vets are usually reluctant to investigate too quickly using this technique, if it is likely that heart failure might be the cause. Finally, there are many causes of weakness or episodes of collapse other than heart disease (see earlier), and comprehensive investigation may be required before the source of the problem can be elucidated.

The clinical examination

The effectiveness of the circulation can be partially evaluated from an examination of the arterial pulse, usually taken at the femoral artery, inside the hind limb. This can be weak if the blood pressure is low, as in forward or low-output failure, or variable in heart dysrhythmias. The colour of the 'mucous membranes' (the gums or the 'pink' or conjunctiva of the eye) is used to reflect whether the small blood vessels (capillaries) have shut down in vasoconstriction, and the state of the jugular veins, which will be distended in right-sided congestive heart failure, are also used to provide clinical information.

The strength of the heart beat can be evaluated by feeling the 'apex beat' of the heart, on the chest wall behind the elbows. As with the pulse, this is related to heart rate, and it may indicate disturbances to the heart rhythm. If there is a large volume of abnormal and turbulent blood flow, or disturbed flow of high energy, a precordial thrill or vibration may be felt.

The chest may be auscultated with a stethoscope to detect the presence of fluid (hydrothorax) which may muffle heart sounds and displace the normal airway breathing sounds. The lungs may also be heard to 'crackle' if full of fluid.

The classic and most useful way in which the heart itself is evaluated is by auscultation with a stethoscope. During this, several features can be evaluated:

(a) *Audibility of the heart*:
Heart sounds may be unusually loud if blood pressure is high, they may be heard over a larger than normal area when the heart is enlarged in congestive failure or they may be muffled by pericardial effusions or fluid in the chest.

(b) *Heart rate:*
This is usually consistently increased in heart failure ('tachycardia') although sometimes it may be excessively slow ('bradycardia').

(c) *Heart rhythm:*
Most normal dogs have regular irregularity of the heart at rest — it speeds up and slows down, usually in time with the breathing. This rhythm, however, is often disturbed in heart failure or myocardial disease but it may also be disturbed by metabolic (chemical) or endocrine (hormone) disorders. The heart beat may be very erratic in heart failure due to atrial fibrillation, especially in large dogs with dilated cardiomyopathy. Minor rhythm disturbances, however, are also common, for example in heart failure due to mitral valve disease.

(d) *The presence of abnormal heart sounds:*
Normally, only two heart sounds are heard in dogs. In overload of the left ventricle, however, especially with cardiomyopathies, a third heart sound may be present. This is heard over the apex of the heart on the left side and is described as a 'gallop' sound. Much more commonly, the abnormal heart sounds heard in dogs are heart murmurs. These are created by turbulent blood flow, typically through leaking heart valves or some congenital disorder such as a stenotic valve, patent ductus arteriosus or septal defect. The character of a murmur can indicate to the veterinary surgeon the type of

underlying heart disease, and to some extent its
severity.

Murmurs can be classified by:

- *Intensity:*
  This is graded on a scale of 1 to 5 or 6 with 1 being
  the softest and 6 being the loudest. Generally, the
  more severe the defect, the louder the murmur,
  although this may not always be the case.
- *Timing in the heart cycle:*
  The murmur may occur during contraction (systole)
  or relaxation (diastole) of the heart and the position
  within the cycle may give guidance as to cause. The
  duration of the murmur is also significant and
  generally the more prolonged a murmur, the more
  serious it is.
- *Point of maximal intensity:*
  The site of the murmur will give a strong indication
  of its likely origin. The murmur of patent ductus
  arteriosus, for example, is found under the left
  forelimb, high up over the heart, whereas the
  murmur of mitral regurgitation is heard behind
  this limb, typically behind the elbow, at the apex of
  the heart. On the contrary, murmurs of tricuspid
  regurgitation or ventricular septal defect are
  generally heard best on the right hand side of the
  chest.
- *Radiation of the murmur:*
  Generally, the more severe the cardiac defect, the
  wider the area over which it may be heard.
- *Consistency:*
  Many, rather insignificant murmurs, representing
  minor disease or even an aberration of normal blood
  flow in young puppies, are often variable from beat
  to beat and according to heart rate, and such
  murmurs may therefore be inconsistently audible.
  In severe disease, however, murmurs tend to
  persist.

Further investigation of heart disease

Although after his clinical examination, the vet may have gained
a reasonable idea of the type of heart disease he is dealing with,
whether it is causing heart failure and its significance to the
patient, certain further investigations may be needed to define

the disorder with much greater certainty and help to determine the prognosis and best course of treatment.

Radiology ('X-Ray')

Chest (thoracic) radiographs are very useful in the identification of congestive heart failure in the dog. They discriminate well between air and fluids and since the lungs are full of air and the heart is full of fluid, they can provide enormous amounts of useful information. However, X-Ray films are photographic negatives and, as in any photograph, any movement can ruin the clarity of the picture. Since the thorax is moving continually as the animal breathes and this cannot be easily overcome, the best chest films are usually taken under general anaesthetic. An anaesthetic, however, often represents significant risk to dogs with heart failure and so it is often considered excessive in relation to the information likely to be obtained. Sedatives can be useful in restraining patients and represent much less risk even in quite severe disease. The use of 'fast' X-Ray screens allow shorter exposure times and so reduces the risk of unexpected movement spoiling the films.

Thoracic radiographs may show fluid in the lungs and overloaded pulmonary blood vessels (pulmonary oedema or congestion) and can show overloading of the other large veins. Sometimes they reveal fluid in the chest (pleural effusion) and they reliably demonstrate enlargement of the heart in congestive heart failure. They are particularly useful in indicating which, if any side of the heart is predominantly enlarged and on which side of the circulation, overloading has occurred. Conversely, if the dog has lost a great volume of fluid, eg as a result of haemorrhage ('hypovolaemia'), the heart and blood vessels may look unusually small.

Although conventional X-rays do not permit the clinician to view structures inside the heart, this can be achieved by using 'contrast' agents which highlight the flow of blood within the heart and blood vessels. This technique is known as angiography. Contrast media (usually solutions that contain iodine) are injected either directly into the heart or major vessels using long narrow tubes (or catheters, see below) or through a needle into a large vein (in the neck or leg). The flow of blood can then be viewed on a special TV monitor or by repeated X-Ray films taken in quick succession. This usually requires specialist equipment and is therefore usually only available in a well-equipped referral centre.

Electrocardiography (ECG) (see page 14)

As discussed earlier, regulation of heart rate and rhythm is under the control of specialist nerves which supply the heart 'pacemaker'.

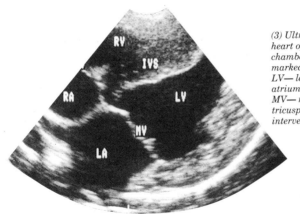

(3) Ultrasound scan of the heart of a greyhound. The heart chambers and some valves are marked (LA— left atrium; LV— left ventricle; RA— right atrium; RV— right ventricle; MV— mitral valve; TV— tricuspid valve; IVS— interventricular septum).

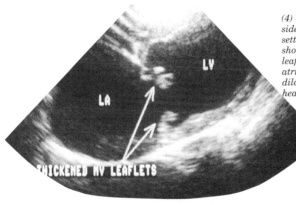

(4) Ultrasound scan of the left side of the heart of an English setter with mitral valve disease, showing thickening of the valve leaflets. Note that the left atrium and ventricle are dilated (swollen) as a result of heart failure.

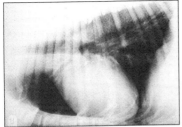

(5) Thoracic radiograph from a normal Irish Wolfhound. The heart is normal in size, and the lungs (black) are clear.

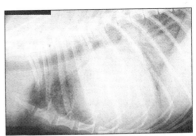

(6) Thoracic radiograph from a border collie with severe pulmonary oedema following heart failure. The heart, is greatly enlarged, and the oedema fluid in the lungs appears as fluffy / streaky white density.

Electrical impulses created by contracting and relaxing heart muscle can be registered by an ECG recorder. ECGs were first used in dogs at the beginning of this century and are now in fairly general use in veterinary practice. By measuring this electrical activity, ECGs display the sequence of the triggering of the heart beat and therefore record the heart rate very accurately. They do not, however, record how efficiently the ventricles are beating and are limited in the diagnosis of congestive heart failure.

ECGs are most valuable for the accurate diagnosis of dysrhythmias (heart rhythm disturbances). Correct therapy for abnormal rhythms is not possible without the benefit of an ECG recording. Sometimes, rhythm disturbances are very intermittent and a single ECG recording, or even repeated short recordings, may fail to identify serious, but only temporary disturbance. In these circumstances, continuous (24-hour) recordings may be required, or an 'event monitor' can be used. With this, 15 minutes or so of ECG can be recorded at will by a supervisor every time a button is pressed to activate the recorder. This can be used for animals displaying episodes of collapse, although the equipment is not widely available and nor does it answer all questions.

ECGs can also give information as to which chamber/s of the heart is/are enlarged and in this they may complement X-Ray films. Finally, ECGs can demonstrate abnormalities that indicate metabolic (chemical) or physical abnormalities in the heart muscle (myocardium) although detection of such changes is neither sensitive nor specific.

Echocardiography (ultrasound scan) (see page 21)

Ultrasound, best known for scanning pregnant women, provides an ideal means of visualising solid structures through fluids and, since the heart is full of fluid (blood), this organ is readily examined using these techniques. Ultrasound scanning provides views of structures inside the heart that conventional X-Rays cannot. Air (as in lungs) and bone (as in ribs) impede ultrasound signals, however, and it is not always easy to find a 'window' between the ribs and under the lungs through which to scan the heart. This is particularly difficult if the dog wriggles or pants. Ultrasound equipment is expensive, and thorough scanning of the heart is a specialist skill requiring considerable training. However, many veterinary practices are now equipped with suitable ultrasound equipment. Ultrasound is a particularly valuable tool because it non-invasive, so minimising interference with the patient.

With echocardiography, the clinician can view structures such as heart valves and identify abnormalities in their shape and function. Congenital abnormalities such as septal defects can be seen and the heart can be measured for enlargement, so allowing identification of any thickening ('hypertrophy') of the myocardium or volume overload (dilation) of heart chambers which may be present in congestive failure. This technique also allows measurement of the strength of contraction of the ventricles. This is very poor (hypokinetic) in cardiomyopathies and is easily recognised with ultrasound, as are pericardial effusions and some (large) heart tumours.

Doppler echocardiography

The Doppler principle states that the frequency (pitch) of sound appears to increase as it approaches and to decrease as it moves away from a listening point. This effect is easiest to understand when we hear the approach and departure of vehicles, sirens, train whistles, etc. By the same principle, the ultrasound signal is reflected by moving tissues in the heart and will increase or decrease in frequency, according to the speed and direction of that movement. As the blood cells represent a large bulk of moving objects within the heart and large blood vessels, the Doppler principle can help the echocardiologist evaluate the speed (velocity) and direction of blood flow anywhere in the heart and large vessels. This is most helpful in detecting the presence and severity of abnormal flow, for example, through leaking valves or shunts. In addition, Doppler can give a very accurate measure of the severity of congenital valve stenosis.

This is another expensive, but very valuable diagnostic tool available to heart specialists.

Cardiac catheterisation

Traditionally, before the availability of ultrasound, diagnostic information from within the heart could only be obtained by passing tubes ('catheters') through the blood vessels into the heart chambers. In dogs, this usually required an anaesthetic which was potentially dangerous in heart disease, and risk was also associated with the catheters themselves in that they could irritate the heart and cause serious rhythm disturbances. The benefit of such procedures was dependent on the accurate placement of catheters in the heart which required specialist X-Ray systems (fluoroscopy) by which the X-Ray images could be seen on a screen, rather than on still films. Catheterisation was therefore expensive, and required skill and equipment beyond the reach of most veterinary practitioners.

As other techniques have become more readily available, cardiac catheterisation is carried out less today than previously, but the information provided can still be of value. This procedure may allow measurement of blood pressure within the heart and large vessels, analysis of intra-cardiac blood gases (oxygen and carbon dioxide), visualisation of structures within the heart by delivering X-Ray 'contrast' materials (angiography), and even the recording of ECGs and heart sounds from within the heart.

Other tests

Numerous other tests may be carried out in the diagnosis of heart disease and include:

(a) *Routine blood samples:*
These may help to identify whether there is any blood cell disturbance, eg anaemia or leukaemia, and to assess the chemical and/or hormone status of the animal.

(b) *Blood pressure evaluation:*
This is much less valuable in dogs than in it is humans. Firstly, the traditional method of measuring blood pressure in humans using an inflatable cuff and a stethoscope does not work effectively in dogs. Secondly, high blood pressure ('hypertension') is much less common in dogs than in humans where it is part of the syndrome which includes coronary artery disease. Hypertension is seen only occasionally in dogs usually with chronic kidney ('renal') disease and it can be measured indirectly from the outside using the tail or the lower part of a limb, or directly by invasion of a needle into a major artery. In both cases, the animal must be reasonably relaxed and co-operative if accurate results are to be obtained.

6 Treatment of heart disease and heart failure

Few heart diseases can be cured and this must be recognised before embarking on treatment. Furthermore, when heart failure develops, although symptoms may be relieved for weeks, months or even years, the disease is often progressive, and end result may be fatal. With careful nursing and modern drugs, however, the lifespan and quality of that life can be significantly improved for most dogs and is therefore usually worthwhile.

When considering treatment, the distinction must be made between minor heart disease with which the animal is coping well, and a degree of heart failure for which the circulation is now failing to compensate. This requires an accurate diagnosis, probably using some of the further investigations outlined above. Furthermore, a detailed discussion of the dog's likely future requirements in terms of management and treatment, and the rationale for selecting therapy should take place between the vet and the owner. For optimal co-operation and the best chance of success, it is best that the owner understands what the vet is trying to achieve.

Specific (surgical) therapy

A few disorders may call for specific therapy. For example, in the hands of a skilled, experienced surgeon, the success rate in tying-off ('ligating') a patent ductus arteriosus is about 95%. Furthermore, this operation should be carried out as soon as the disorder is diagnosed (often at the time of puppyhood vaccination) and before irreversible heart disease has developed, even if the dog appears to be well at the time. Some degree of success in relieving the effects of pulmonic stenosis can also be achieved by surgery or the use of a balloon catheter. Sadly, the results of similar techniques for aortic stenosis have been far less successful so far. Successful valve replacement has been achieved experimentally in dogs but current techniques are far too expensive and the long-term results too unpredictable for routine use.

Other disorders for which specific therapy can provide permanent improvement include some pericardial effusions. Drainage of pericardial haemorrhage by the use of a catheter or cannula passed across the thorax into the pericardium can be successful in many cases. Even if haemorrhage recurs, surgery to open the pericardium, and to permit drainage of the blood into the thorax, may give permanent relief of heart failure if no tumour is present.

Treatment of Congestive heart failure

The choice of therapy for congestive heart failure is likely to be similar, almost whatever the cause. As in most cases of heart disease, the value of adequate rest in relieving congestive failure cannot be overemphasised. Were many dogs affected with heart failure to receive total rest (eg confined to a kennel all day), it is likely that the signs of heart failure would disappear without medication. There has to be a compromise, however, between the dog's quality of life and medication required and this should be weighed up when long-term treatment is being discussed. At the very least, dogs with congestive failure should have exercise partially restricted. Every time the dog takes exercise, his kidneys are effectively being 'starved' and so function poorly. Owners often imagine that the dog will limit its own exercise but this is seldom so and some dogs with heart failure will die while at exercise. What may not be so obvious is that some hours after exercise, a dog's breathing or coughing may be worse as a result of fluid retention brought about by the period of impaired kidney function.

Congestive heart failure brings about the retention of fluid and sodium at the kidneys, while the dog continues to absorb salt (sodium chloride) from the diet. For this reason, some experts recommend dietary sodium restriction for dogs with impending or actual heart failure Most commercial dog diets contain far more sodium than is required even by the normal dog, let alone an animal with heart failure. Salt is included to increase palatability. Prescription diets specifically formulated for dogs with heart failure are available through vets, although their poorer palatability as a result of low salt content may not be tolerated by an ill dog. Furthermore, while the level of sodium in these restricted diets may be adequate for a dog in heart failure, medication may include drugs which increase sodium loss through the kidneys and lead to sodium depletion. The value of these diets is therefore debatable, and is yet unproved.

Diuretics

The mainstay of therapy for congestive failure are diuretics. These drugs increase urine production, usually together with sodium loss, which can relieve very effectively (but not cure) the effects of congestive failure. When on such medication, it should be understood that through increasing urine production, the dog will drink more than before, and there is a likelihood of 'accidents' through the dog being unable to retain its urine throughout the night. Since these drugs usually begin to take effect in the first hour after giving the tablet and may continue to be effective for some 6 hours or so, it is wise to consider the timing of treatment so as to minimise this risk.

Commonly-used diuretics are frusemide (eg Lasix, Diuride, Frusid, etc.) and the thiazides (Saluric; Vetidrex). One or two additional agents are used occasionally (amiloride and spironolactone) but only in cases of chronic or persistent oedema and usually in combination with others. Diuretics are generally very safe, and to some extent, the dosage can be adjusted according to the animal's response to therapy. Coughing, heavy breathing and abdominal swelling due to ascites may all show considerable improvement with diuretics. True toxic effects are few, although excessive dosage can lead to dehydration, despite persisting signs of oedema, whereby excessive reduction of the fluid volume load to the heart may impair the heart's function.

Digitalis glycosides

Extracts of Foxglove (Digitalis purpurea) have been used for the treatment of human heart failure for over 200 years, and they were mentioned by Blaine in his textbook on treatment of dog diseases early in the 19th century. They are potentially very poisonous, however, and should only be used under very strict veterinary supervision. These agents have two main functions. They improve the contractility of the ventricles (strengthen the heart beat) and control the heart rate when too fast, as is often the case in congestive heart failure. In many cases however, the strength of the heart's contraction is quite adequate until relatively late in the progress of the condition, in mitral valve disease, for example. Glycosides are used predominantly to treat heart failure when there is loss of strength of the heart beat, such as in dilated cardiomyopathy in large dogs. These dogs also often have atrial fibrillation with an excessive heart rate which may also be controlled by these drugs.

Glycosides include digoxin (Lanoxin), the drug most frequently used, and digitoxin. The dose for any individual dog is very variable. Some dogs such as Dobermans appear to be far more sensitive to their effects than others, and dogs absorb the drug variably. Furthermore, the toxic dose of these drugs is not very much higher than the effective dose: the 'therapeutic margin' is very narrow. Monitoring of blood samples for drug levels can help in verifying the correct blood levels and ensuring they remain safe and effective. When given daily, digoxin builds up ('accumulates') in the body over about 5 days so it is from this stage that toxic signs might be expected, although they can also occur after months of use. Signs of toxicity and actions to take should be well understood by any owner administering glycosides to their dog. With glycoside toxicity, the dog may become lethargic and depressed within hours. The dog will refuse food, and it is likely to vomit. Later this may be accompanied by diarrhoea. If dosing is continued for a day or so after this stage, death may ensue. It is clear therefore that should any of these signs be seen whilst being treated with these drugs, administration should be stopped immediately and veterinary advice sought. Nonetheless, when the body has had an opportunity to eliminate excessive drug after two or three days, treatment can be resumed at a lower dose. Digoxin can also be irritant to the stomach lining, which can cause sickness soon after dosing, in the absence of true toxicity. In these circumstances a different formulation such as an Elixir can be tried.

Several other agents may be used to increase the strength of the ventricle's contraction: these include caffeine derivatives (xanthines), and drugs such as milrinone, which has been shown to be effective in dogs. Milrinone has been shown to increase the quality of life in human patients with heart failure although with an accompanying decrease in survival rate. Dobutamine may also be effective in increasing the strength of ventricular contraction. This drug is given by intravenous drip to dogs with very severe heart failure such as Dobermans with cardiomyopathy.

Vasodilators

In heart failure, the small blood vessels (capillaries) tend to tighten ('vasoconstriction') so as to ensure that the impaired circulation reaches the vital organs. While this is a good mechanism for maintaining blood pressure in severe fluid loss, it means that a failing heart has to beat against a high resistance if it is to maintain the viability of all body tissues. This has several detrimental effects on the heart and circulation. Firstly, the ventricle, which may be already failing, has to work harder and consume more energy. Secondly, the increased pressure in the circulation will exacerbate valve leakage. These factors, despite the extra effort of the ventricles, give rise a reduction in the forward flow of blood from the heart ('cardiac output') so that some peripheral tissues (including the muscles and kidneys) may have their blood supply further reduced. Because of the reduced cardiac output and venoconstriction, pressures in the main veins are still high which 'squeezes' fluid from the circulation into the tissues, including the lungs. Vasodilators, therefore, in dilating the peripheral blood vessels, reduce excessively high blood pressure ('hypertension') and reverse many of the effects described above.

Several types of vasodilator have been developed for human

use including: hydralazine; angiotensin-converting enzyme (ACE) inhibitors; antagonists to the 'alpha' effects of adrenaline (eg prazosin), and nitrates. As many of these agents are relatively modern drugs, they tend to be rather expensive and most are not yet licensed for use in dogs.

Hydralazine has been shown to be an effective arteriolar vasodilator in heart failure in dogs especially when failure is associated with mitral valve incompetence. However, the smallest tablet size is large for a dog, it may cause loss of appetite and vomiting, and can lead to a sudden loss of blood pressure and collapse. Although this collapse unlikely to be fatal, it can be alarming to the dog's owner. This drug is not yet licensed for dogs and is not widely used.

ACE inhibitors are now being used routinely for the treatment of congestive heart failure in dogs, especially with disorders such as the common mitral valve disease and dilated cardiomyopathy. Enalapril (Cardiovet) and benazepril are licensed for this purpose, and other similar agents may soon be granted a veterinary licence. Enalapril has been shown to improve quality of life and to prolong life significantly in dogs with heart failure. Clinical trials reveal improved activity, alertness, appetite, breathing, and reduced coughing as a result of treatment without the occurrence of significant side-effects. The beneficial effects of ACE inhibitors appear to be maintained even to the extent that continued improvement, particularly in exercise tolerance, over weeks or months. Furthermore, there may be some beneficial effects on the heart muscle, and ACE inhibitors are, themselves, mild diuretics. As described above with hydralazine, the occasional dog may collapse whilst on treatment but this is a feature of most vasodilators by virtue of their mode of action. As with diuretics, this can precipitate kidney failure in a dog with pre-existing renal disease.

Captopril was in use before enalapril, but this drug seems to cause more side-effects (eg inappetance) in dogs and is, as yet, unlicensed for veterinary use.

Nitrates, such as glyceryl trinitrate (nitroglycerine — eg Percutol), besides being potential explosives, are dilators of small veins (venodilators) and coronary vessels. In humans they are often used for angina in coronary artery disease (rare in dogs), being sucked or kept under the tongue in response to an attack the drug is absorbed from the mouth. Venodilation, as opposed to arteriolar dilation, is most helpful in cases of severe pulmonary oedema (fluid in the lungs). A resultant fall in pressure on the right side of the circulation (in the veins) allows an increased withdrawal of blood from the congested vessels in the lungs. This can produce a rapid response. However, since dogs cannot be asked to suck tablets and since this drug is absorbed and excreted too quickly to remain effective if swallowed, veterinary preparations are usually rubbed as an ointment or applied as a patch onto the skin. In applying ointment, however, people treating dogs should be careful to wear gloves or they themselves will absorb the drug.

Sodium nitroprusside, a very potent drug, is also occasionally used in dogs, but this must be given under close supervision of blood pressure whilst the animal is under intensive care.

Other vasodilators, such as prazosin have been used with some success in dogs, but the beneficial effects of this drug appear to wane after a few weeks.

Treatment of severe pulmonary oedema

Severe flooding of the lungs in heart failure is potentially life threatening and it requires very prompt therapy if the dog is to survive. Several courses of action may help to relieve the oedema.

Firstly, coupage may be used: In this, the dog is held up by its hindlegs, and the chest pummelled to help to drain the airway (trachea) of accumulated fluid that is blocking it. Secondly, oxygen can be given, preferably by constructing a tent of oxygen-enriched air for the dog to breathe or by placement of a small tube (catheter) through the nose, into the throat, and securing it to the nose with 'superglue'. Trying to enrich the oxygen intake by placing an oxygen mask over the nose as would be adopted with human patients is resented by most dogs, and their struggling exacerbates the condition. Thirdly, nitrates may be given, as above or fourthly, frusemide may be given intravenously. Not only does frusemide act very rapidly, but it also acts as a venodilator (see above) when given directly into the blood stream. Fifthly, morphine may be given for its sedative properties and for its beneficial effects on the overloaded lungs. In addition, the general treatment for congestive failure described earlier may be tried, along with glycoside and xanthines medication. If pulmonary oedema is recurrent, clients may wish to retain some nitroglycerine for emergency use, although continuous use probably leads to a diminished response.

Treatment for coughing

Dogs with chronic mitral valve disease often cough badly. This requires therapy for small airway disease as much as for heart failure. Firstly, the dog should be treated as for congestive heart failure, with diuretics and vasodilators. Secondly, drugs that dilate the smaller airways (bronchodilators) may be helpful, as in human asthma, and these include the xanthines (caffeine derivatives). Like coffee, these are mild stimulants of the heart and the brain, and they are mild diuretics, but they also help to relieve coughing. Drugs commonly used include aminophylline, etamiphylline (Dalophyline, Millophyline) and theophylline (Corvental-D). These agents can be irritant to the stomach and occasionally cause the dog to be hyperexcited, but they are neither very potent nor very toxic. Thirdly, treatment for coughing may include cough suppressants such as the morphine-derived codeine or butorphanol (Torbutrol) which may help to relieve coughing, particularly if this is very irritating to dog or, indeed, the owner. Finally, general treatment for small airway disease ('chronic bronchitis') may help.

Treatment for bradycardias

When the heart's own pacemaker beats too slowly, this is sometimes due to excessive stimulation of the vagus nerve by the autonomic nervous system. In such cases, the use of vagal inhibitors such as atropine may be employed. This is another very ancient drug ('belladonna': so called because it was employed by ladies to dilate the pupils of their eyes to make them appear more beautiful). As well as speeding up heart rate however, atropine has a number of undesirable side effects such as blurred vision and drying of the eyes, mouth and nose, which cannot easily be described by dogs! This drug is related to some of those used to prevent travel sickness in humans. Another similar agent is glycopyrrolate.

Whether or not an excessively slow heart rate responds to therapy, treatment often fails to prevent episodes of collapse. Often, the only solution to a persistent and significant bradycardia may be use of a heart pacemaker. This procedure has now been available for dogs for more than 15 years. Modern pacemakers are sophisticated pieces of equipment which monitor and respond to the patient's heart activity. Only when the heart is too slow does the pacemaker trigger, and the rate at which it stimulates the heart to beat can be pre-programmed. Some pacemakers may even increase the rate of 'pacing' when shaken, so that the heart rate increases while the dog is at exercise. This saves the battery, and it allows more 'normal' heart function in tune with the dog's activity.

Pacemakers are usually fitted under the skin of the neck, or inside the abdomen. A connecting wire or 'lead' runs from it to the heart and conveys the electric signal which controls the heart rate. This lead is either placed into the right ventricle through the jugular vein, or screwed into the outside surface of the right ventricle through a surgical incision into the chest. This latter method is potentially dangerous when there is 'heart block' and this technique is now usually avoided. Scrupulous hygiene and sterility are vital in this operation if complications are to be avoided, and it is usually only available at specialist centres such as universities or referral clinics. Pacemakers are prohibitively expensive for veterinary use and as a result, either shelf-life expired units or units removed from humans and re-sterilised are used. Despite this, the price of the lead, surgery and ancillary equipment means that the procedure costs several hundred pounds.

Although a solution to episodes of collapse, pacemakers are not ideal, as the heart is activated from the ventricle, rather than the normal pacemaker site. It is very difficult to provide the ideal heart rate for every type of activity — from sleep to exercise — with a pacemaker. They may, however, save the dog from sudden death or premature heart failure and can give a very useful extension to life.

Treatment for tachycardias

When the heart rate is persistently too fast (tachycardia) (typically more than about 160 beats per minute in dogs), specific therapy should be considered. If the heart rate exceeds 200 beats per minute for more than one month, an otherwise healthy dog is likely to develop congestive heart failure due to deteriorating cardiac output. Furthermore, excessive tachycardia should always be controlled, not only because of the likely development of cardiac failure but because tachycardias or irregular premature beats may precede cardiac arrest.

Many of the agents that can be used in the treatment of tachycardia have side-effects such as a potential to cause a more severe rhythm disturbance ('pro-arrhythmic' effect). Furthermore, few studies have been made in dogs to determine which drugs are most effective, which rhythm disturbances should be treated, or whether successful treatment prevents further cardiac deterioration and arrest. Much treatment has therefore to be used on the basis of experience, and trial and error. Whatever the specific disturbance, the dog should be checked very carefully for chemical (metabolic) or physical disease that may be stimulating the dysrhythmia, and, the specific nature of the tachycardia or rhythm disturbance should be determined by ECG before starting therapy.

Tachycardias arising from above the ventricles (supraventricular tachycardias) require the use of therapeutic agents rather different from those used for ventricular disturbances. Three main types of drug may be used, the cardiac glycosides (eg digoxin — see above), beta adrenergic blockers or calcium antagonists ('calcium channel blockers').

Beta blockers inhibit some of the 'sympathetic' effects of agents like adrenaline, which include tachycardia, increased force of ventricular contraction and high blood pressure. They are therefore mainly effective for tachycardias (atrial or ventricular) in which sympathetic activity plays a part. The dose at which they may control the heart rate in any individual animal varies, and determination of the correct dose is sometimes difficult. Beta blockers are, however, relatively safe agents, although care has to be taken not to reduce the heart rate too much.

Typical beta blockers used in dogs are propranolol (Inderal), which is rather short-acting (in dogs) and atenolol (Tenormin) which is a longer-acting agent. To ensure that the tachycardia under treatment is sensitive to beta blockers, esmolol (Brevibloc) can be used as an intravenous injection by which it acts for only 15 minutes. One of the main drawbacks with these drugs (and a number of other drugs used to treat tachycardias) is that they may further decrease the force of contraction of a heart that is already failing. This may cause the animal to be very weak and/ or to exacerbate any heart failure.

Calcium antagonists prevent the entry of calcium, essential for the contraction of heart muscle, into the muscle cells. They can therefore slow the activation of the heart, but may also reduce the strength of contraction. Examples of calcium antagonists include diltiazem and verapamil (Cordilox). Calcium antagonists should be used with care if combined with glycosides (eg digoxin) and the dose of glycosides reduced.

For ventricular tachycardias, the agent most usually effective is lignocaine, better known as a local anaesthetic (eg used by dentists). However, this drug is active for less than an hour and it must be given intravenously — either as a single dose or as a continuous drip. Other agents must therefore be used to follow up successful therapy with lignocaine. There is a derivative that can be given by mouth: tocainide (Tonocard). This is less likely to be effective, however, and over a long period of time it has caused keratitis (damage to the cornea of the eye in dogs). More reliable, cheaper and less likely to give side-effects, is procainamide (Pronestyl), which has been used for many years in dogs. Other similar drugs such as quinidine sulphate and disopyramide are more likely to cause vomiting and/or diarrhoea, a potential side-effect of most of this group of therapeutic substances. Other less-commonly used drugs include amiodarone and bretylium.

None of these oral agents will reliably control tachycardias, and sometimes a combination of drugs, eg together with a beta blocker may be needed.

As well as by the use of drugs, occasionally supraventricular tachycardia can be terminated by one of two nerve reflexes. This can be pressure on the eyeballs or pressure on the 'carotid sinus', found in the area of the throat.

Treatment for cardiac arrest

Cardiac arrest is most likely to occur when there is already serious heart disease and/or the dog develops some chemical (metabolic) disturbance or if there is a lack of oxygen (hypoxia). Furthermore, as there are several different rhythm disturbances that can be present at cardiac arrest which cannot be differentiated without ECG and because cardiac arrest often takes place in an animal already seriously ill, an ideal protocol for resuscitation cannot be given. Even in the best regulated circumstances (human intensive care), the proportion of victims of cardiac arrest successfully resuscitated is low. Nevertheless, more people should be trained to attempt cardiac resuscitation in humans and animals, and trained as a co-ordinated team. The longer any attempt is delayed, the less successful it is likely to be. For a simple step by step approach, see Appendix A.

Product Group	Examples	Mode of Action	Conditions Treated
Diuretics	h'chlorothiazide* frusemide*	Remove fluid from the circulation	Congestive heart failure
Digitalis Glycosides	digoxin digitoxin	Improve contractility of the ventricles, slow the heart rate (vagal action)	Cardiomyopathy and tachycardias
Vasodilators	enalapril* benazepril*	Dilates peripheral blood vessels so as to reduce the effort the heart requires to move blood	Congestive heart failure
Xanthines	etamiphylline* theophylline*	Cough suppressant	Cardiac associated coughing
Beta Adrenergic Blockers	propanolol atenolol	Inhibit the effect of adrenaline on strength of heart contraction and blood pressure	Abnormally high heart rate (tachycardia) and excess hypertrophy
Calcium Channel Antagonists	diltiazem verapamil	Inhibit the passage of calcium into the heart muscle cells so slowing the rate and strength of cardiac contraction	Abnormally high heart rate (tachycardia)
Local Anaesthetic	procainamide tocainide	Inhibits neuromuscular transmission	Ventricular tachycardia

Drugs used in the treatment of cardiac disease in dogs

*These products carry a Veterinary Product Licence

Appendix A

Step by step approach to cardiac resuscitation

A classic approach is to consider A-B-C-D-E-F:

Airway

The airway should first be established, by drawing the tongue forward, extending the neck and removing any obvious obstruction.

Breathing

Artificial respiration should then be practised, by mouth-to-mouth or by pressing regularly on the chest.

Circulation

The circulation can be assisted by attempting to pump the heart through the chest wall between assisted respirations. The circulation is also assisted by binding the hind limbs and the abdomen tightly.

If a veterinary surgeon is attendance, then continue to D, E and F

Drugs

Drugs such as adrenaline can then be given: this is best given through the airway but it is often injected into the heart.

Electrical activity

An ECG should be checked to ascertain the rhythm disturbance, and electrical defibrillation used if necessary.

Follow-up.

If resuscitation is successful, then the patient should be monitored intensively.

Glossary

ACE inhibitor	angiotensin converting enzyme inhibitor — a vasodilator used in the treatment of cardiac failure
anaemia	reduced number of red blood cells
angiography	visualisation of heart using special dyes and X rays
aorta	major vessel taking blood from heart to the arterial system
apex beat	beat of the heart felt on the side of the chest
arrhythmia	loss of normal heart rhythm
ascites	abdominal collection of fluid
atrium	collecting chamber of the heart
autonomic nervous system	nerves which control unconscious processes (eg the heart beat)
auscultation	listening with a stethoscope
bella donna	plant from which atropine is extracted ('deadly nightshade')
bradycardia	slow heart beat
bronchi	major airways produced by dividing of the trachea
bronchodilation	widening of the small airways
calcium channel blockers	drugs which inhibit the movement of calcium into heart muscle cells
capillaries	smallest of the blood vessels
cardiac output	the amount of blood being pumped around the circulation by the heart
cardiomyopathy	heart muscle disease
catheterisation	passage of small tube into an internal structure (eg blood vessels)
compensation	change in function in attempt to maintain adequate circulation of blood
congestive heart failure	impaired cardiac output giving rise to accumulation of fluid in the circulation and tissues
contrast media	materials used to highlight tissue on X ray
coupage	draining airway by holding dog up by back legs and pummelling the chest
cyanosis	blue tinge produced by reduced oxygen content of blood

dehydration	abnormal reduction of fluid content of the body
diastole	relaxation phase of heart between beats
dilated cardiomyopathy	disease seen mainly in large dogs — heart muscle becomes flabby (loses its strength)
distended	over-filled
diuretics	drugs which increase urine production and body fluid loss
doppler echocardiography	non-invasive procedure used to examine blood flow in the heart
dropsy	see ascites
ductus arteriosus	vessel which by-passes the lungs in the foetus
dysplasia	abnormality of development
dyspnoea	difficulty in breathing
dysrhythmia	heart rhythm disturbance
ECG	electrocardiograph — used to monitor electrical activity of the heart
echocardiography	procedure using ultrasound to study cardiac function
ectopic beats	extra beats arising from out with the pacemaker
endocrine	involving hormones
escape beat	'rescue' rhythm from outside the pacemaker
fibrillation	rapid random writhing (of heart) when control of pacemaker is lost
fluoroscopy	X ray technique where moving image can be seen on a monitor rather than on a film
gallop beat	extra heart sound which occurs in some kinds of cardiac disease
haemorrhage	blood loss from the circulation
heart block	impairment of electrical impulses from pacemaker to heart muscle
heart rate	number of beats/minute
hole in the heart	see *septal defect*
hydrothorax	collection of fluid in chest cavity
hypertension	high blood pressure
hypertrophic	increase in size (or thickness) of heart muscle
hypoglycaemia	reduced blood glucose

hypokinetic	decreased activity
hypovolaemia	reduction in circulating fluid
incompetence	impaired function (or leakage throught heart valve)
inhalation	breathing in
left to right shunt	movement of blood directly from high pressure left heart to right eg through ventricular septal defect or patent ductus
lesions	site of pathological abnormality
ligating	tying off
metabolism	the physical and chemical processes which allow the body to function
mucous membranes	surfaces of the body which secrete mucus eg gums, conjunctiva etc.
murmur	abnormal heart sound as a result of abnormal blood flow
myocardium	heart muscle
myocarditis	inflammation of heart muscle
neoplasia	tumour or cancer
oedema	accumulation of fluid
oesophagus	gullet
pacemaker	area of the heart which control electrical activity of the heart and so heart rate
pericardial effusion	accumulation of fluid in pericardium
pericardium	bag surrounding the heart
pleural effusions	accumulation of fluid in the chest around the lungs
precordial thrill	abnormal vibration of heart which can be felt on the chest wall
premature beats	additional and abnormal heart beat
pro-arrhythmic effect	propensity to cause arrhythmia
prognosis	anticipated outcome
pulmonary	accumulation of fluid in lung tissue
radiology	x ray study (eg chest)
receptors	areas which receive chemical messages and so produce physiological effect

regurgitation	abnormal flow (of blood) eg through leaky valve
renal	pertaining to the kidney
right to left shunting	movement of blood directly from right heart to left eg through ventricular septal defect with pulmonary stenosus
seizures	fits
septal defects	hole in the wall between two sides of the heart
sinus arrhythmia	regular irrecularity in electrical control of heart rate (found in many normal dogs)
sinus node	true pacemaker of heart electrical activity which controls electrical impulses
pacemaker	see *sinus node*
stenosis	narrowing of opening
systole	contraction phase of heart beat cycle
tachycardia	increased heart rate
therapeutic margin	difference between dose required to produce desired effect and that which is toxic
thorax	chest
ultrasound	very high frequency sound emissions used to examine (scan) internal organs
vagus nerve	major nerve of the autonomic nervous system which has the effect of slowing the heart.
valves — atrioventricular/ mitral/tricuspid	flap which between vessels and/or chambers of the heart so as protect heart from high pressure during diastole
vasoconstriction	narrowing of blood vessels
vasodilation	widening of blood vessels
venodilators	dilators of small veins
ventricle	large powerful pumping chambers of the heart
ventricular fibrillation	rapid randomised writhing of ventricle common form of cardiac arrest
volume overload	excess accumulation of fluid in the circulation
xanthines	caffeine derivatives — used to treat some kinds of heart disease